Empath and Psychic Abilities

Discover the Secrets of Psychics and Empaths. Develop Abilities Such as Intuition, Clairvoyance, Telepathy, Aura Reading, Healing Mediumship, and Connect Your Spirit Guides

Chakra Power

Empath and Psychic Abilities

© Copyright 2021 - All rights reserved.

The content contained within this book may not be reproduced, duplicated or transmitted without direct written permission from the author or the publisher.
Under no circumstances will any blame or legal responsibility be held against the publisher, or author, for any damages, reparation, or monetary loss due to the information contained within this book. Either directly or indirectly.

Legal Notice:
This book is copyright protected. This book is only for personal use. You cannot amend, distribute, sell, use, quote or paraphrase any part, or the content within this book, without the consent of the author or publisher.

Disclaimer Notice:
Please note the information contained within this document is for educational and entertainment purposes only. All effort has been executed to present accurate, up to date, and reliable, complete information. No warranties of any kind are declared or implied. Readers acknowledge that the author is not engaging in the rendering of legal, financial, medical or professional advice. The content within this book has been derived from various sources. Please consult a licensed professional before attempting any techniques outlined in this book.
By reading this document, the reader agrees that under no circumstances is the author responsible for any losses, direct or indirect, which are incurred as a result of the use of information contained within this document, including, but not limited to, errors, omissions, or inaccuracies.

Empath and Psychic Abilities

Table of Contents

INTRODUCTION 8

CHAPTER 1: A COMPLETE GUIDE TO PSYCHOMETRY 10

- What is Psychometry? 10
- A Brief History of Psychometry 12
- How to Know If You Have Psychometric Abilities? 14
- 3 Kinds of Psychometry 16
- How Does It Work? 18
- Practicing Psychometry 19
- Using Psychometry 22
- How to Do a Reading? 24

CHAPTER 2: IMPORTANCE OF SPIRITUAL QUOTIENT 28

- How Did This Term Originate? 29
- Aspects of Spirituality 29
- Difference Between EQ, IQ, and SQ 30
- 12 Principles of Spiritual Intelligence 32
- Importance of SQ 41

CHAPTER 3: HOW TO RECOGNIZE IF YOU ARE AN EMPATH? 44

- What is a Psychic Empath? 45
- Types of Empaths 48

Emotional empath 49

Physical empath 50

Claircognizant empath 51

Psychometric empath 51

Earth empath 52

Telepathic empath 53

Intuitive empath 53

Medium empath 54

Dream empath 55

Precognitive empath 56

Geomantic empath 57

Plant empath 57

CHAPTER 4: UNDERSTANDING YOUR ENERGY AS AN EMPATH ... 60

How are Empaths More Sensitive than Others 61

Understanding Empath Energy 67

Understanding Empath Fatigue 68

Tips to Overcome Empath Fatigue 71

Get to know yourself 71

Invest in self-care 72

Learn to create boundaries 74

Identify your triggers 75

What goes in also goes out 76

CHAPTER 5: EVERYTHING YOU NEED TO KNOW ABOUT PSYCHIC PROTECTION 80

   Centering and Grounding Exercises 82

      What is Grounding? 83

      How to Ground Yourself? 84

      What is Centering? 84

      How to Center Yourself? 86

CONCLUSION 90

Empath and Psychic Abilities

Introduction

Keep in mind that sympathy and empathy are two different things, even though people tend to get confused between the two. They are often used interchangeably even when their meanings are different. Sympathy is simply the other name of pity, but an empath walks that extra mile to understand why someone is behaving the way they are behaving, and they do everything they can to alleviate other people's pain.

But empaths need to nurture their quality in order to truly be able to use it to the best of their abilities. On top of that, if you are a psychic empath, it will be even harder for you to spend your day-to-day life because you can literally feel all the energies surrounding you. But in this book, we will learn how you can prevent yourself from getting overwhelmed by emotions and how to practice greater control over life, in general.

There are plenty of books on this subject on the market; thanks again for choosing this one! Every effort was made to ensure it is full of as much useful information as possible, please enjoy!

Empath and Psychic Abilities

Chapter 1:
A Complete Guide to Psychometry

A very important part of enhancing your psychic abilities is learning psychometry, and we are going to discuss all aspects of it in this chapter. In brief, psychometry is the art through which a person can automatically understand or 'read' an object's history by simply touching it.

They either touch it to their forehead or hold it in their hand. Any kind of touch gives them impressions about the object. These impressions can be in the form of sounds, smells, images, emotions, or even tastes.

What is Psychometry?

Psychometry is a special ability through which people can practice seeing things that are not usually seeable in the real world. It is often referred to as the psychic way of seeing. Different people see in different ways. Some people use the surface of the water, black glass, or a crystal ball – everyone has their own ways. The main characteristic feature of psychometry is that people can practice this extraordinary talent through touch.

A person who has psychometric talents is often referred to as the psychometrist. Let me give you an example of how it's done. Suppose you give them an antique watch, and they hold it in their hands. They can tell you all about that watch and who owned it with their power of touch. They might even be able to tell you about the different experiences the person had when they had that watch in their possession.

You will be surprised to know about the different things the psychic can tell you – they can give you a hint of what the person who possessed the object was like, what they did in their lifetime, or even how they died. But among all of these things, the most important thing that the psychic can tell you is how that particular person was feeling at a certain point of time in their life. It is said that an object can very strongly store a person's emotions in them, and thus, even psychometrics can sense it very easily.

You must keep in mind that a psychometric might not be able to display the same level of seeing/reading with all types of objects. The accuracy of their psychic abilities differs from one object to the other. Most people get confused about the basic idea of psychometry – it is not focused on the future but on your present and past. That is how it differs from a typical crystal ball reading.

The concept of psychometry and the term itself was coined by Joseph Rhodes Buchanan, an American physiologist and physician.

He explained psychometry with the example of geologists. Just like geologists study the past from the fossils, psychometry is related to 'mental fossils.' An object gives off a certain energy, which is then used to study the science and history of the human mind.

Essentially, psychometrists are of the belief that each and everything on this planet has a soul, including objects. They acquire a memory based on how a person is interacting with them. A person can figure out the history of that object or its owner if they are sensitive enough to feel the energy emanating from these objects.

A Brief History of Psychometry

In the year 1842, Joseph R. Buchanan was the person who coined the term 'psychometry.' The word is derived from two Greek words – psyche and metron. Here, psyche means 'soul,' and metron means 'measure.' Out of all the experiments conducted with psychometry, Buchanan was one of the first to do so, and he was an American physiology professor. He kept different types of drugs in glass vials.

After that, he asked his students to hold the vials and identify what kinds of drugs have been kept there through the power of touch. It was more than chance that they succeeded, and the results of this experiment were published in his book – Journal of Man. To put it in a brief sentence, Buchanan explained this phenomenon, saying that all objects have the ability to retain a memory because they have a 'soul.'

After that, William F. Denton started his own experiments in psychometry after being inspired by the works of Buchanan. Denton was an American geology professor, and his aim was to make sure whether the concept of psychometry works on the geology specimens he works with.

He then invited his sister, Ann Denton, to help him out in his experiments in the year 1854. He took a piece of cloth and used it to wrap around all the geological specimens he wanted to test. This ensured that Ann couldn't see what the specimens were. Ann took the package and touched it to her forehead. She received very clear mental images, and with their help, she was able to describe all the specimens correctly.

Then came Gustav Pagenstecher, who carried out work on psychometry from 1919 to 1922. He was a psychical researcher and a doctor of German origin. In between these years, he discovered that one of his patients possessed psychometric abilities.

The name of the patient was Maria Reyes de Zierold. Maria could prominently talk about the past of an object and its present by simply holding it, during which she also entered a trance-like state. She could state the experience of the object in this world and go on describing smells, sounds, sights, and several other feelings.

So, based on this observation, Pagenstecher had formed a theory that every object has certain vibrations condensed into it, and if a person can tune into those vibrations, they can learn about the experience of that object.

How to Know If You Have Psychometric Abilities?

With all this talk about psychometry, I'm sure you are very excited to know whether you have psychometric abilities or not. Well, in general, it has been noticed that most psychometric readers are empaths. The tendency is even more strengthened if you have the skill of clairsentience to a reasonable level.

But, for a better idea, if you want to know whether you have psychometric skills or not, here are some signs that you should look out for –

- You feel a strong vibe from antique stores, or they simply make you feel weird.

- When there are too many objects in a space, you feel uncomfortable because many objects mean too much energy.

- You only use new furniture. Used furniture makes you feel uncomfortable.

- You cannot wear used jewelry or someone else's clothes.

- If you have picked up any used object, you have this impulse at the back of your mind to immediately wash your hands.

- You feel overwhelmed while visiting pawn shops.

So, have you been experiencing any of the signs mentioned above or anything similar to that? If yes, then there is a high chance that you will excel at the psychometric skill.

All of these signs show that a person is ready to read the energy in an object and even explain what the object has gone through.

In fact, psychometric skills can even help you figure out why you hate certain objects in your life, like, your uncle's couch.

3 Kinds of Psychometry

Now, let us have a look at the three kinds of psychometry that is there –

Object Psychometry. It is the type of psychometry that most people know about and is the most popular out of all three. Like I mentioned before, there is a certain amount of energy present in all objects of earth. The owner who had that object with him/her leaves behind a unique imprint on the object.

People who practice object psychometry work towards establishing a solid rapport with the item/object they are working with. They also work on building a close relationship with the energies that have been imprinted inside the object. There are three different ways in which you can read the imprints in any object –

- By holding the object in your hands
- By placing the object against your face or forehead
- By placing the object against your solar plexus

When you place the object in either of the above-mentioned ways or make contact with it, you will get an idea about the history of the object or its owner through the impressions.

Location Psychometry. This type of psychometry is very similar to what we commonly refer to as déjà vu. In short, even when you haven't been to a place, and you get this sensation that you have been there, it is referred to as déjà vu. It also has similarities with different forms of diving and dowsing, for example, finding out the feasibility of mining in a place by attuning to one of the ore samples.

Some traces are left by incidents in the location they happened. This is even truer for strong and emotional events. These locations get imprinted with the energy of that event. And thus, you can read these imprints.

Person Psychometry. This type of psychometry relies on the idea that there is an energy field surrounding everyone on earth. Almost all people implement this psychometry method. Have you ever encountered a situation where you were able to assess a person's mood without even speaking with them? I'm sure you have. Then, there is another very common example – every time you meet someone new, you are either repelled by them or attracted to them. This is also because of person psychometry. There is no complete explanation of how these impressions work, but every person will vouch for the fact that they have a strong effect.

How Does It Work?

Out of all the explanations, researchers have paid extra careful attention to the vibration theory proposed by Pagenstecher. Psychics have always claimed that the vibrations from an object are conveyed to them, and these vibrations are imbibed in that object through actions and emotions that were accumulated in the past.

Keep in mind that the concept of messages being conveyed through vibrations is not your regular New Age talk. There is a substantial scientific basis too.

Michael Talbot wrote a book called *The Holographic Universe,* and in this book, the author has stated that the past is never really lost. In fact, some form of human perception always keeps the past alive.

Talbot used the scientific knowledge that vibrations are exuded by all forms of matter on earth at a subatomic level. Using this information, he stated that "reality and consciousness are present in a type of hologram where a record of past, present, and future exists.' It is the power of this record that psychometrics can use to their advantage.

If you consider the literal meaning of the term 'psychometry,' it comes down to measuring a soul since 'metry' means measuring something, and 'psych' refers to the soul.

So, people who have the special gifts of psychometry and have mastered the art implement their extrasensory talent to study the objects and understand the energy that is coming out of them. It can even be described as an energy signature. Every object tries to tell its own story through its energy signature. As you all know, most people who have psychometric abilities are also empaths by nature – this means they can guide others by understanding their emotions and energy.

I have heard from most people that the easiest reading experience they had was with metal objects, but if you practice enough and master the art, you can read just about any object with equal expertise. In fact, if a person is very sensitive to energy, they can even pick up signals if a person's photograph is shown to them. This is also the basis of online psychometric readings where the reader cannot meet the person face-to-face.

Practicing Psychometry

Have you ever been to a second-hand store or an antique shop and got a weird feeling? Or, did you ever feel a bad vibe from a piece of rental furniture for absolutely no reason at all? If this has happened to you, then there is a high chance that you have the ability to perform psychometric readings because you are very sensitive to the energy around you.

All those weird sensations or feelings that you experienced are because of the energy that is given off from the things around you.

It can be quite overwhelming for sensitive people to be around shared objects or older items usually found in hotels or flea markets because they have more energy stored in them because of the multiple owners they have encountered in their lifetime.

All of these different people have imbued the objects with their own energy, and so when you come in contact with them, you might be sensing and picking up some conflicting auras and energy.

No matter what, you should always keep in mind that psychometry is not exactly backed up by science. People use their individual talents of intuition and other gifts to sense and understand the energies coming out of objects.

Every person's method is different from that of the other. For example, some might be picking up an emotion while others might rely on some vision or a particular smell.

If you want to practice psychometry yourself, here are some steps that you should follow –

- **Select a space where you can think without any disturbance.** Thinking with clarity is always the first step. Choose an environment that helps you concentrate on thinking. For example, you can close the shades, play some music you like, or light a candle.

- **Relax.** The importance of relaxation in the process of psychometry has been confirmed by several famous psychics around the world. They claim that it helps you enter a sort of trance state and achieve a much higher level of consciousness. So, it will, in turn, help you form a stronger connection with the object that you are trying to analyze with your psychometric abilities.

- **Touch the object or hold it in your hands.** Pick up the object in your hands or touch it. Another thing that you can do is ask someone else to place the object in your hands.

- **Explore your feelings or sensations.** Start feeling the energy that the object is emanating. Allow yourself to pick up on the energy. Whatever you start feeling or thinking comes from your intuition and is usually correct. In fact, at times, you might also find yourself experiencing intense emotions and visualize complete images in your mind.

- **Say what you are thinking.** Sometimes people assume that what they are thinking is meaningless or trivial and so they don't say anything. But you shouldn't do that because you never know what might be significant for the object you are reading.

Using Psychometry

Scrying and psychometry have some noticeable similarities between them, but at the same time, there are some differences as well. When you psychometrize an object, you delve into the astral vibrations that it is emanating.

You first hold it in your hands and keep cradling it while you sense the vibrations. After that, you can pass it from one hand to the other and then even turn it around in your palms. Your awareness of the object and its energy will keep increasing the more you increase your contact with it.

When you finally enter this state of tranquility and ultimate relaxation, you let go of your analytical thinking and allow your reflective capabilities to start acting. This gives your consciousness a free pass to receive the sensations from the astral vibrations of the object. This type of reading is purely instinctual in nature.

After a while, when you are further into this relaxed state, you will feel an increase in the flow of the energy, and this increase will allow you to receive the signals in a passive manner. It's like you keep listening as the object keeps talking. The psychic material starts forging its own course, and you enter a state where you are 'dreaming awake.' The stages keep unfolding in a progressive way. In fact, some people compare this process of psychometry with that of the water lilies and how they grow. The concept goes something like this – the lake with its placid and serene water resembles your mind, and the water lilies represent the material bound by psychometry. Here, the lilies blossom from the depths of the lake into consciousness, just like your mind.

Similar to scrying, there are various forms in which the object can present itself to you – it can be feelings, ideas, or mental imagery. But whatever it is that is coming to your consciousness – you should say it out loud and verbalize it. So, even if you are alone and practicing psychometry, this is a good way of doing it. The vibrations are interpreted by when your mind delves deeper into your unconscious mind. The predictions are even truer when they arise from the depth of your consciousness.

Your proficiency in predicting the astral vibrations will keep on increasing as you make further progress into the art of psychometry. With time, you, too, will improve.

How to Do a Reading?

Just like any other skill, the more you practice, the better you will become at giving readings. With practice, it will become easier too. Psychometry can be mastered by anyone as long as you can display the right amount of empathy.

So, while performing a psychometric reading, here are some of the basic steps that you need to follow –

- The first step is to wash your hands with water. Then, dry them completely. This step ensures that all the residual energy in your hands is washed off, but you don't need to be hospital sterile for this. Once the existing energy is washed off, it will no longer interfere with your readings.

- Now, create some warm-up energy by rubbing your hands together. This energy is created through friction.

- The next step is to check and understand whether some energy has been created or not. For this, start by placing your palms in a way that they are facing each other. Now, start pulling them apart. Remember that you have to pull them apart by approximately a quarter of an inch. Do you feel any energy or some weird sensation between your palms? If you do, then energy is present, and you are all set to do a reading! But if not, then it means that you have to rub your hands a bit more, and energy will be created.

- Now, take the item you want to read in your hands. It is always advisable that you begin your reading with something that is more of the personal kind and is a small object. For example, a piece of jewelry that holds sentimental value is a good place to start. For beginners, it makes it easier to go past the initial exercise. Another thing to keep in mind is that it would work well for you if the person whose belonging you are using is not someone you know closely; for example, you can ask one of your family friends to lend you a family heirloom jewelry for a couple of days.

- The next step is probably the most important one – you need to relax! Take whatever measures you need to for this – you can even choose to close your eyes.

- Now, open your mind and allow thoughts to come in. Allow the feelings, emotions, images, and memories to come into your mind because these are being sent by the energy that is stored in the object. So, what are you sensing – taste, smell, see, or hear?

I am listing some very important questions that you can use during psychometric readings –

- Who does the object belong to?

- Can you sense the personality of the owner after holding the object?

- What are the experiences or memories that the owner had while they had the object with themselves?

- Has the owner passed away, or is he/she still alive?

Empath and Psychic Abilities

Chapter 2: Importance of Spiritual Quotient

In previous times, people used to consider only a person's IQ as a valid mode of intelligence that could be acknowledged and respected at the end of the day. But fortunately, time and people changed for the better over time, and it was during the 1990s that people started grasping the concept of emotional quotient or emotional intelligence. It became common knowledge over time that how people deal and conduct their emotional intelligence could be as important and at times more so than their intelligence quotient. Some more years passed, and the concept of measuring one's intelligence in ways not prescribed by society started becoming more acceptable to people, and it was during the 2000s that people came face to face with the concept of spiritual quotient and its different facets.

The question that arises then is what exactly this spiritual quotient is. What is required is to understand it completely and how someone can truly exercise it in their day-to-day lives. Another set of questions that emerge naturally out of this is that if a spiritual quotient is really a form of intelligence, then, like other forms of intelligence, can it be used to fight problems like terrorism or psychological problems, say insensitivity?

How Did This Term Originate?

Danah Zohar and Ian Marshall can be attributed to coining these terms "Spiritual Quotient" or "Spiritual Intelligence," which are based on their path-breaking book which is called "SQ: Connecting with Our Spiritual Intelligence." Danah and Ian, while describing Spiritual Quotient, tells us that it is the most fundamental of all our intelligence, and it is our spiritual quotient that helps us develop the inner capacities in us of value, meaning, and that of vision—allowing us to strive hard and giving us the passion and courage to dream. Our values always play a role in any action that we take, and that is perhaps the reason our spiritual quotient helps us to explore the beliefs and values in us so that we can live up to our full potential and our lives can become much more satisfying and worthy.

Aspects of Spirituality

1. **Responsibility** – It is very important for every one of us to have some purpose in life because, let's face it, we are not going to be around forever. That is why it becomes imperative to use every moment that we have

at our disposal in ways that could be helpful for us and meaningful for everyone around us. We need to realize that we have come here on earth with certain responsibilities towards ourselves and others and need to accept and respect those responsibilities.

2. **Humility** – It is very important for everyone to realize that we are just one among the 7 billion people who inhabit the earth. While it is important to know one's worth, it is also important to maintain a certain level of humility at all points because only if we can give other people their due respect will we be able to give ourselves the respect that we deserve.

3. **Happiness** – We need to find out for ourselves what exactly happiness means to us. It is a concept that has no fixed definition. It depends from person to person, and it is upon us to find out all its connotations and work hard towards actualizing that in our lives.

Difference Between EQ, IQ, and SQ

1. **IQ – Intelligence Quotient** basically refers to the attempts that we make to measure human intelligence. Every human being has their respective cognitive strengths as well as weaknesses, but psychologists have found out that there is one common component among

us all known as the general intelligence or G. this can be beautifully defined in the words of Robert Feldman, "the capacity to understand the world, think rationally and use resources effectively when faced with challenges."

2. **EQ – Emotional Quotient** can be defined as the ways that we choose for ourselves to manage all our emotions in a positive manner so that no matter what situations we might face in life, we should be well equipped emotionally to deal with them. In the mid-1990s, Daniel Goleman came up with this, and it has been revealed through proper studies that those people with a higher EQ find it easier to deal with any kind of situation than those whose score is less. People with a higher emotional quotient understand their own emotions better and thereby can deal with their own psychological situations maturely. Things like managing stress and dealing with conditions like depression can get a lot easier if the concerned person's EQ is high.

3. **SQ – Spiritual Quotient** is something that we need to go beyond our cognitive and emotional skills if needed to be understood. It is that understanding present deep within us that makes us realize that we are, after all, mortals, and so, we need to do our best to make our existence worthy by offering something fruitful and helpful that could be helpful for others. It paves the way

for acceptance of one's weaknesses as well as achievements and to live a life of humility and respect. It also helps give things and people their necessary importance and balance work, personal life, and inner growth.

12 Principles of Spiritual Intelligence

Each of us has been endowed with these three above-mentioned kinds of intelligence, and it depends on us as to how we use them to our advantage while dealing with any kind of situation in life. Some of us have been equipped with more of one of these, but they are all present in us. They can be fostered in us individually as per need. And as per as spiritual quotient is considered, there are twelve principles that can be looked at in order to foster it properly. Let us look at them in detail.

Both physically and mentally, we all are consciously an adaptive system, so we hope to build flexible collaborations that will have dialogues with the environment around us. The principles that will be discussed now are great modes of such collaboration that will be underpinned by values, vision, meaning, and purpose.

- **Self-Awareness** – It has to be kept in mind that that spiritual self-awareness is different from the otherwise self-awareness that we know, which is basically having an idea about one's own thoughts and feelings at a given point in time. Spiritual self-awareness is being aware of what an individual feels, what an individual loves and cares for genuinely, and what they live for in life. Spiritual self-awareness also encompasses those things that an individual feels so connected with that they can even die for. Being spiritually self-aware is to remain true to oneself and others around. Only if we are remaining true to what we live for will we be able to communicate honestly with our deeper self. When that communication becomes strong, our communication with the outer world becomes strong as well.

- **Spontaneity** – It is not only enough to do whatever you feel at that point in time. It is equally important to do that work with self-discipline, self-control, and practice. Being spiritually spontaneous implies that we will be emotionally capable enough not to let our emotional baggage be a burden. Be it our childhood problems or some prejudices that we might be having, or be it even certain assumptions. We should be capable enough to regard things and situations for what they are and be responsive accordingly. Most importantly, we should be able to take proper responsibility for all that we do.

- **Being Vision and Value-Led** – It becomes essential to lead a life that has its values set based on a positive vision. Every work that we do, every action that we take should have a purpose to it. A purpose that makes it worthy of being done or thought of. Our life should also be like that, a life that is worthy and has the vision to strive for. We should have certain reasons for whatever we do. Be it education or job. It shouldn't be restricted to completing that one exam or reaching that one profit margin. We need to constantly ask ourselves questions like "what is the purpose that I want to achieve with my education?" or "what help will it be to the world if I reach this profit margin?" only when we are led in life by a vision, will our lives have any value.

- **Holism** – If we take quantum physics into consideration, holism could be defined as a system so integrated that each part needs to be defined with respect to the other parts. If we put this definition into a real-life perspective, we will find out that each and every one of us is defined in terms of others. That we are existing is bound to be related with others that we are in direct contact with. For example, if we take a speaker who is giving a speech to a large audience. At that point in time, the existence of that speaker is true only because there is an audience listening to him at that point. The relevance of the audience is also true because the speaker exists. This was a simple way of getting a broader picture of what Holism is. The faster we realize this, the better for us because only then will we be able to work in harmony as a whole.

- **Compassion** – Spiritual compassion will help you feel what the other person is feeling and act accordingly. It is not only enough to recognize or just to accept what the other person is going through. Only when you make an effort to actually feel what the other person is going through will it become easier for everyone to lead a much happier life or, for that matter, a much more respectable life. Compassion makes you and others become human beings who lends a hand to those in need, and it is always a joy to be around such people, to know that there are people who, instead of trying to judge you or take advantage of your situation, is willing to help you and support you mentally.

- **Celebration of Diversity** - It is extremely important to respect differences and celebrate the diversity around, because everyone and everything matters, even at times when things are always not in line with what we feel. Celebrating diversity is important because that teaches us what actually matters and that this world and our society have a lot more to offer than what we might think. Let us think this through for a moment. Most of us have had the opportunity to grow up in an educational environment where we had classmates from all sectors of society, from different classes of economy, catering to different religious beliefs.

- This is one of the most necessary things that every child should experience, as this will teach a child from the very beginning that nothing matters other than one's own deeds and values. Where they come from should be the least of our concerns because what matters is where we are going. This feeling is intimately related to compassion.

It is really a beautiful emotion to be able to celebrate the differences in people so that as a society, we can rejoice in every aspect of human life that we have. So that instead of focusing on things that are problematic, we can rejoice in things that are beautiful and that will bring joy in everyone's lives.

As human beings, it is our responsibility to accept the fact that not everything will be the way we want to, and at the same time, it is necessary to understand that others' opinions are not wrong. Getting to know new things will invariably broaden our horizons and open our minds to a bigger and better world.

- **Field Independence** – Field Independence is actually a very simple thing if you understand it properly. It basically means having the courage to stand up for one's beliefs and focus on what you actually want rather than getting scared or persuaded into what others are trying to believe. It is basically to have the courage to stand in front of a host of people and say what you have to, not lose your ground and not let anyone force you into believing something else that you otherwise wouldn't have. It also means to not be unaware of what others have to say, listen to them properly, consider their points carefully, and not get easily swayed away. It is a stable balance between not disregarding others and, at the same time, not giving in easily.

- **Humility** – Humility is like being on the other side of the spectrum from field independence. It is to understand that no matter what happens, you have got to keep your head about things and not sit on your high horse all the time. As important it is to stand your ground about the views that you have of things, it is important to not disregard others and accept the faults you have any. If you feel like you are lacking somewhere and have committed any mistakes, then it is best for you as well as for others with whom you are interacting. If you accept those mistakes and instead of wasting time, work hard on correcting yourself and the situation. In life, there will come many people who will know more than you. It is only natural to feel intimidated by them. But let that situation turn into an unpleasant one. Use it to your advantage to learn and better yourself.

- **Tendency to Ask Fundamental "Why?" Questions** – Anyone who is aware of how this world works knows this basic thing that none of us are born with all the knowledge, and none of us can ever match up to the limits of knowledge that is available to us. So, if we think that what we know is enough, then we are wrong. There is always something more than what meets the eye. If we are to truly enlarge our horizon, we simply have to get into the habit of asking such "why?" questions. "Why is it that I have to be a part of this?", "Why is this thing done this way and not the other way round?".

At an initial stage, it might feel a bit silly to ask these questions, but, in the long run, we will be in a position of advantage as we will slowly become more insightful. This habit of asking questions and not taking things for granted or at their face value is sure to make us into more inquisitive individuals who are emotionally more prepared to grasp things than others who are not so flexible in their approach.

- **Ability to Reframe** – It is essential to have the sensibility to look at what you have done objectively and, if need be, to change things when the time is right. Mind you. It is not easy to do this because not everyone has the courage to reframe. But, for those who know, understands how essential it is to detach yourself from your work for some point and look at it from a neutral point of view so that you can see for yourself what mistakes you have made and what are the things that need to be changed. You have to make this into a habit to take some time off at regular intervals and look back at what you have done so far. It is bound to be beneficial for everyone if this process is to be followed. This makes you always keep your feet on the ground and become aware of your mistakes. At the same time, it helps you always be prepared for changes. It keeps you updated with recent trends and makes your work much more relatable and contemporary.

- **Positive Use of Adversity** – At every point in time, life teaches us something new. It gives us reasons to go ahead and improve ourselves. It also teaches us that we are, after all, only humans, and it is alright to make mistakes. What life also teaches us is that the problems we face can all be used in a positive way if we have such a mindset. All the adversities that we face teach us many important things, and all we need to do is keep a close eye on them. Firstly, we need to analyze why did we face that adversity in the first place.

I am sure that we will find some definite reason for that. We need to avoid those the next time. Secondly, we need to do a thorough search of what exactly did this teach us and make sure we use that detail to our advantage the next time.

- **Sense of Vocation** – The sense of vocation as a principle helps in summing up our spiritual intelligence with our spiritual capital. At present, it usually refers to practices such as medicine, law, and teaching. If a business becomes a vocational practice, it will invariably cater to a larger audience, and it will start having a nobler purpose, helping a larger community of people.

The word vocation comes from the Latin word "vocare," which translates to "to be called." Initially, it referred to the practice of a priest calling out to God. It got its new connotations recently.

As it has the capacity to reach out to a larger audience, it is sure to be of great help to many. So, if your spiritual quotient has the sense of vocation embedded in it, you are sure to become a source of aid for people around you.

Importance of SQ

Spiritual Quotient helps a person enhance their insight and their creative abilities. What is interesting to know is that, unlike Intelligence Quotient or Emotional Quotient, Spiritual Quotient helps a person deal with modern problems like inconsiderateness or even terrorism. Already emerging as the next huge thing for scientific consideration, Spiritual Quotient helps us deal with problems like lack of humanness which directly relates to a person's psyche like human awareness and human consciousness.

The spiritual quotient has the capability to recognize intelligence and senses that are beyond the five senses that we have. The universal power responsible for governing everything that happens within and without us, and this power is omnipresent. We are required to surrender to this power with all our awareness. Our spiritual quotient helps us understand all these things in greater detail so that we can get in touch with the core of strength that resides within us. That, in turn, helps us to balance the powerhouse without us, ensuring that there is a sense of harmony in the world and in our environment. It becomes easier to deal with the ups and downs and live a happier life.

Even the corporate world, which is devoid of emotions and feelings per se, has a lot of use of this spiritual quotient because no matter how professional that work sector is, it ultimately deals with human beings. It is not humanly possible to treat them like robots, with emotions and feelings, and then to expect them to garner good results. For any person to give their best in their work and at the same time for any workspace to have positive energy, it is important for everyone around and involved to have a healthy and spiritually progressive environment.

Empath and Psychic Abilities

Chapter 3:
How to Recognize If You Are An Empath?

As social beings who are dependent on social interactions and emotional connections among us, we all experience and possess the feeling of empathy towards others, only varying in degree from people to people. We may relate to it as kindness, and almost all of us strive to become a person who is kind, who cares about and considers the feelings of other people. Empathy is, as defined by Webster's New World Dictionary, "a feeling, emotional or intellectual identification with another." The ability to understand the experiences and feelings of others outside of an individual's own perspective is known as empathy.

For example, say that your friend is going through a loss in the family. In such a scenario, it is empathy that allows you to understand the pain that your friend is going through and the emotions that she is dealing with, even if the situation and the circumstances are completely different from where you stand and what you are feeling. However, that is not all. As an empath, you take all of this a little further. An empath actually senses and feels these emotions that the other person is feeling as though it is their very own.

If we explain in simpler words, it can be said that as an empath, someone else's pain or happiness or anger becomes your own pain, happiness, and anger. Empaths are hypersensitive people who are able to understand, feel, tune in to, and resonate with the feelings of others around them. This can happen voluntarily, but sometimes, this becomes the case even involuntarily.

What is a Psychic Empath?

While all of us strive and work towards becoming a better version of ourselves filled with kindness and understanding of those around us, some people are born with abilities beyond normal, ordinary kindness that we know of. Such people have the ability to connect and resonate with the emotions and feelings of other people on a very deep and powerful level that is beyond normal capabilities.

Do you often feel an instant connection with the feelings and emotions of other people around you, like your friends and family, even when you are in a very different emotional state altogether? Let's dive into what psychic empathy truly is, how it works, and what it means. This will help you recognize and understand your own nature and abilities.

Empathy, as discussed earlier, is the ability to identify, understand, and feel sympathy towards the feelings of other people. The term psychic empath is derived from empathy itself and is used quite frequently to refer to a psychic individual who is intensely sensitive and receptive to other people's feelings, emotions, and energies that they experience all these emotions as though it is their own. The term psychic empath is becoming more and more popular and common in the psychic and the paranormal realms. This is because psychic empaths have the ability to probe deeply into the soul of another person and help them to identify and experience the feelings and emotions that may have been blocked. They display profound sensitivity to the emotional states of both themselves as well as others. Having said that, sometimes, it is even possible that the emotional states of others may overpower their own emotions as they are barely able to distinguish their own feelings from someone else's. There is always a probability that the empaths themselves are not aware of their abilities and may just refer to it as being super sensitive around others.

There is a distinct difference between what empathy is and what psychic empathy is, and it is very important not to get these two confused. Empathy is a human emotion that exists in all of us in varying degrees, and we all are able to connect and sympathize with people and their feelings. Psychic empaths, on the other hand, have an extrasensory perception that is above normal human empathy. Psychic empaths can easily detect and identify the feelings and emotions of people around them, and they can pick these up on non-visual, non-verbal cues. They just know what people are going through and the emotions they are feeling regardless of the fact whether that person is letting out his/her feelings at all or not. Therefore, they feel the moods, intentions, and motives of other people unconsciously. Some psychic empaths can even feel the emotional impact that is radiated by people, animals, and even plants in the surrounding environment and even the universe. While everybody who has healthy emotional states is able to feel empathy, psychic empaths have the ability to experience the emotions of others directly.

In addition to that, a psychic empath also differs distinctly from a traditional psychic as the former does not have the ability to sense, see, hear, or read into the spiritual realm or get glimpses of the future possibilities; rather, they are able to read and identify emotions. They have the ability to instantly enter into another person's aura. They can connect with the feelings and emotions the other person is feeling deeply and can understand their life experiences almost instantly and very intimately. However, similar to other psychic abilities, an individual may be born with it, and this ability is often known to be multi-generational. But, it is believed that a person might be able to obtain this ability after a near-death experience. This is not a confirmed statement open to debate, but this is widely believed.

Types of Empaths

Some psychic empaths have the ability to sense the emotions and how others are feeling by tapping into their aura or energetic vibrations, while others, on the other hand, are able to use a unique ability known as Claircognition to simply "know" the emotions and the underlying feelings of a person without having any obvious verbal, vision, or any type of clue.

If you feel like you can instantly connect with someone's feelings on a personal and deep level and even feel very overwhelmed when you are in a crowd full of people due to their emotions draining your energy, you might be a psychic empath yourself. From empaths who are physical to emotional empaths, from earth empaths to animal empaths, there are several types of empaths present. These differences come forward due to the different types of ways through which they obtain information. Each one of these empaths has distinct abilities. Here are the main and most common types of psychic empaths that may help you recognize which one is you:

Emotional empath

As depicted by the name, these types of psychic empaths experience the emotions of others. It does not matter whether or not the people in question are related to these empaths or not.

They may feel the sorrow of a fellow passenger who has just lost his pet, or the excitement of someone on the street who has just passed the interview, or the joy of the family that is expecting. These emotions do not necessarily have to be exhibited to be felt by the emotional empath; they just feel these emotions even if they are well hidden inside by these people.

However, as shown in the example above, this ability has both pros and cons as the empath may suffer the pain of someone who is suffering while they can also rejoice in the joy of someone else. This type of empath may feel emotionally drained by the negative and narcissistic emotions that they may feel as the day goes on.

For example, the emotions of people who suffer from low self-esteem and always find themselves in crisis mode, seeking constant validation and reassurance can negatively impact the emotional well-being of the empath as well.

Physical empath

Physical empaths have the ability to experience the physical ailments of those around them. They respond to the physical symptoms and actions of people around them. Therefore, when someone is laughing or crying and expressing their emotions physically, the physical empath is most likely to mirror these actions regardless of whether you are experiencing these emotions yourself. Likewise, if you are around people who are suffering from illness or having some kind of body ache, you might experience similar discomfort as them. This ability has a lot of negative impacts on the well-being of the empath as it is obviously not delightful to experience the physical pain of someone. Hospitals prove to be a dreadful place to these empaths, as this generally happens when they are in the vicinity of injured people. However, in some cases, this can occur even across the further distance between the empath and the sufferer.

Due to all these negative impacts and effects, it becomes very important for the empath to train and concentrate on coping mechanisms. This is a major problem surrounding the physical empaths as they unconsciously manifest the physical symptoms of others onto themselves; therefore, it is important and helpful that they are surrounded with healthy and happy people most of the time so that these negative effects are set off. Another very important strategy that might help you if you identify yourself with one of these types of empaths is that you should set healthy boundaries with people and learn that it is okay to say "no" to spending time with people who will add to your stress levels.

Claircognizant empath

These types of empaths have the ability to identify and understand the true nature of any given situation or thing. They are able to instantly recognize when someone is lying or is misleading, and similarly, they always just know the ruth without any logical base. Not only that, they have the ability to know what is to be done and what is important in any situation. Due to this profound ability, the claircognizant empaths are the ideal people to turn to whenever faced with a crisis. The hallmark characteristic of this psychic ability is the empathetic ability to feel relaxed and at peace even when they face a crisis situation.

Psychometric empath

Psychometric empaths have the ability to receive impressions and even decode them, receive information, and on the whole, energy from physical and inanimate objects and even places. Some examples of these are jewelry, homes, pictures, piece of clothing, and so on. The information that they perceive and receive can be in the form of emotions, images, sounds, tastes, etc. A psychometric empath has the ability to know about the history of the object and receive information about an object by simply touching the object. After they have made physical contact with the object, they are able to get information about the owner of the object, the owner's life, the past of the object, and even the experiences that the owner had during the time he had been using or wearing that particular object.

Earth empath

Earth empaths are empaths who are in tune with nature and the environment. They possess the ability to feel and connect with the world and the universe as a whole. For instance, a forest fire can cause them to feel pain, and further, they are even able to sense earthquakes and severe storms even before it happens. These can come as physical symptoms. These symptoms and the sensations they feel before a natural calamity depends on the empath themselves and the disaster that is making its way. As an outcome of feeling and resonating with the earth, they feel calm, relaxed, and in peace after the disaster has passed. Earth empaths rejoice in being outdoors amongst nature, and they thrive when they experience the miracles of nature and are among the natural energy sources. Earth empaths get energized when they see a beautiful sunrise, waterfalls, and other natural beauties. However, the negative impacts of pollution and environmental toxins can cause detrimental effects to them that are heightened than other normal human beings.

Telepathic empath

Telepathy, as most of us know, is a communication type that operates from mind to mind. The information is sent from the mind of a sender to another person who is the receiver without any verbal communication whatsoever. Telepathic empaths, therefore, as the name suggests, have the ability to read the thoughts of others accurately. They can tell what others around them think, including people, animals, even plants and trees.

Intuitive empath

Similar to emotional empaths, intuitive empaths also connect to the feelings and emotions of the people around them.

However, there is more to that in these types of empaths as not only do they pick up on the emotions of others, but they also have the ability to see what truly lies underneath the feelings and emotions on the surface. They go beyond these emotions to see what lies underneath. They sense what is being hidden, unspoken, and not expressed. Most of the time, this type of empath also has the ability to understand whether a person is being truthful or is lying. Intuitive empaths are hence, good judges of character who can find out when someone is not being honest and can therefore find out the reality and truth in every situation.

Medium empath

Also known as mediumship, these types of empaths are quite different from the rest as their ability differs and helps them to sense, i.e., hear, feel, etc., the presence and the energies of the spirits of even the deceased individuals. They are even able to consult spirits or other supernatural beings.

They can see the past, present, and even future events of someone else. They can do so as they receive this information by tuning in to the energy that is surrounding the person in question. While it sure sounds fascinating and maybe a very useful ability, being a medium empath is not easy at all. They are known to be very sensitive to the environment and are often prone to contacting allergies without any known reason and/or show physical symptoms that are inexplicable.

Another drawback that is believed to be associate with medium empaths is that they may not always be able to work to their optimum level as the energies and the field they work in are very sensitive. To further elaborate, no matter how much they are willing to try and help you, sometimes they may not be able to do so for everyone, sometimes they may not be able to solve their own problems. It is a very important step for psychic empaths to learn to differentiate and shield themselves from others' feelings as a means to avoid the bombardment of information all the time upon themselves. If you relate to this type of psychic empathy, it is important that you learn to differentiate between your own feelings, emotions, and senses than that of the others.

With enough practice and patience, a psychic empath should be able to tap into their abilities when in need and then switch it to the background when they are getting on with other things in life. However, because it is such a sensitive ability and, as mentioned earlier, it is not at all easy for medium empaths, sometimes, even with these shielding techniques, they need considerable time alone to shake off the emotions and keep themselves emotionally balanced.

Dream empath
To normal humans, dreams can be very difficult to make sense of, but empaths of this type are very gifted when it comes to unraveling the mysteries of the subconscious mind. Dream empaths are able to remember their dreams vividly and in detail without even missing the most minute detail. They do not forget their dreams as soon as they wake up, as many normal humans do. Therefore, as they remember these details, they acquire knowledge and understanding about the situations that are going on in their lives and the solution as to what should be

done. These dreams give them wisdom. Not only do they have the ability to bring clarity and solution to their own lives, but they also help other people to decipher the meaning behind their dreams and how it may apply to real-life situations helping them find clarity.

Dream empaths can go beyond physical reality and are able to dream of the intuitive information from the universe while they sleep.

Precognitive empath

These types of empaths are blessed with the ability to strongly feel an event or circumstance that is bound to happen. Often, they receive premonitions as to what is going to happen that may manifest as dreams, or even sensations, both emotional and physical, and visions.

They have the ability to sense or receive some form of warning before something dreadful takes place. Precognitive empaths often feel the feeling of incomprehensible doom. Developing and coping up with this ability might take some time and patience.

However, it makes a huge difference and helps if an empath is able to use this ability to make the right decisions and avoid potential threats.

Geomantic empath

Geomantic empaths are very well accustomed to the environment and even the energies of the world. They have the ability to identify and read signals from the energy transmission of the air, water, soil, even rocks.

The skills they possess come in very handy when detecting bad weather conditions, underground water, or any possible natural disaster. A very good example of such empaths would be animals.

Animals are aware of the natural calamities before they happen, and therefore they know when to hide in times of tsunami, flood, etc.

Plant empath

Just as emotional empaths and physical empaths are able to connect to other people and their feelings, plant or flora empaths are known to form similar connections with plants. They are always in tune with the flora around them, such as the trees, flowers, etc.

They are said to even be able to communicate with the plants, can hear their thoughts, and understand them. Therefore, they always know just what a plant needs to be healthy. Not only that, as they are one with the flora around them, they have the ability of healing and herbalism. Not only do they communicate with plants, but this spiritual connection can also be carried to form human connections as well.

Empath and Psychic Abilities

Chapter 4: Understanding Your Energy As An Empath

If you often feel like you are strongly impacted by the energy emitted by people and spaces, then there are high chances that you might be an *empath*. An empath would also feel drained, exhausted, and burnt out if they do not get adequate time in between social gatherings and events because that way, they would be denied any time to recharge themselves. Empaths are also often moved by things like films, novels, or music – all of which makes them experience emotions far more deeply than an average person would.

Due to a high perceptive intuition and feelings, empaths are more prone to feeling emotions in their own body with a higher intensity – both about themselves and other people. Being an empath is quite common. But if you are an empath, you also need to understand how your thought processes are wired so that you are equipped to take proper care of your mind and body while also channeling your empath energy in a better, more meaningful way. In this chapter, we will quickly go through different ways in which you can better understand empath sensitivity and empath energy and the fatigue that can arise from being an empath, and various ways in which they can be tackled.

How are Empaths More Sensitive than Others

Here are the ways in which empaths are considered to be more sensitive than other people around them.

They have a hyper-perceptive emotional system: Most empaths have quite a highly perceptive emotional system, which impacts how they pick up on external energy and react to them. This means that they are more attentive to what is happening around them when compared to other people, which is why they feel drained if they do not give themselves enough time in between different social scenarios and interactions.

Empaths need to regularly recharge themselves as they are not just receptive to what people around them are feeling or doing but also to the collective energy of places altogether, increasing the emotional load they have to deal with. This is mostly a reason why normal tasks, like attending a Zoom call or doing grocery might turn out to be more taxing for empaths, as they need to not just act on how they are feeling during the activity but also need to be mindful about the energies given out by other places and people.

Their physical body and energy are also more sensitive: Besides having a highly sensitive emotional system, they are also physically more sensitive to external energy- both individual and collective. This also means that they would feel external sensations- such as those from caffeine, alcohol, or other substances- a lot more strongly than the people around them. They can also be more sensitive to physical sensations such as a change in temperature or any sort of loud noise, or any other disturbing sensation in their surroundings.

Since each empath is different when it comes to how they respond to external energy, it is natural that they also have different thresholds for physical stimuli, and this threshold keeps changing depending upon the circumstances that they are put in. prolonged exposure to any kind of physical stimuli can also sometimes numb an empath to how they react to the stimuli.

For example, if they find themselves really bothered by how noisy their workspace is, they might eventually get used to it and stop feeling as disturbed as they do in about six months.

They need to actively learn and practice how to tune others out: Since an empath is naturally more wired to what other people are feeling, it might come in handy for them to learn how to tune others off sometimes and be mindful about it as well. For a lot of other people, blocking someone off from your mind might not feel like a very difficult task and would not even take a lot of conscious efforts, but for empaths, it is an important process of self-care and self-recharge to tune others out after a point and tune back into their feelings once the empaths feel more in control of the situation and more capable of dealing with the emotional overload.

While connecting with others at ease is a greatly beneficial quality, it can also get really overwhelming if there are no restraints put upon it, as everyone- including empaths- comes with only limited pools of energy at the end of the day.

They appear to be naturally more kind and compassionate than others: As the name itself suggests, an empath is someone who can feel other people's happiness or discomfort as if they were their own feelings. This naturally makes them kinder, more caring, and more compassionate people, as they have an increased ability to place themselves in others' shoes and understand what someone else is going through without necessarily having gone through the same.

Since empaths feel a lot and are not always able to control how much they should feel for others, if they do not properly connect with their energy, it might become difficult for them to prevent burnout. Therefore, it is important for empaths to show compassion to themselves as well. Sometimes, they need to put themselves and their needs before others. This is because if they get too caught up in the emotional experiences of others, they would not be able to devote a lot of time or effort to control their own emotions. This might leave them feeling bitter and frustrated at times.

In order to avoid these negative feelings of burnout, empaths must develop effective strategies to process their own emotions and prioritize them over other's feelings at all times. Keeping themselves emotionally grounded can also help them in establishing boundaries about emotions so that their own emotional burdens do not spill into others' feelings, and vice versa, and they can deal with all the feelings in their own space and time.

Their energy is easily affected by physical spaces: If you are someone who is usually morse 'picky' about places, then you might actually be an empath and are only drawn towards places whose energy matches with that of yours. A lot of empaths usually prefer clean, organized, and tidy spaces.

This is because their physical surroundings have a great impact on them and their energy. An empath can simply walk into a room and feel a sense of energy – positive or negative – which greatly affects how they interact in and to that situation.
If you are an empath, it might be a good idea to inform your friends, partners, or roommates how you like your spaces to be maintained and how sensitive you are to changes in these spaces so that they can be aware of the relationship between your empath energy and your physical environment, and can help you out with how you try to manage this relationship. Other than physical spaces, empaths can also be sensitive to the energy of different kinds of virtual and digital spaces.

They are easily receptive to collective energy: Since empaths are highly perceptive, they are more open and sensitive to collective energy. This collective energy could mean anything, spanning from a park to a town or even a culture. The empath could be receptive to the collective energy in many ways- they can be exposed to the energy both indirectly (by reading on the news about an event that has happened somewhere far away) or directly (by coming in physical contact with space; for example, by taking a walk or shopping at a crowded market).

To keep a check on how they are being exposed to this energy and how they can react to it, it might help empaths to work on developing certain daily, weekly, and monthly grounding practices and then build a routine around all of those. These practices- such as meditating every morning, meeting your loved ones for dinner every month without fail, or listening to a particular podcast or reading a book- will help an empath feel stable and will foster a sense of regularity and routine in their lives, so that their energy stays under control and does not deflect due to the impact a strong sense of collective energy might have on them.

Other than that, empaths can also channel their sensitivity to collective energy to bring about a positive, impactful change. A lot of empaths are inspired by this sensitivity to become activists and other kinds of changemakers. On the other hand, empaths can also actively seek the type of energy they want to feel and use that to make themselves feel more at peace or more lively, depending on their mood.

They find themselves to be the strongest in the clairsentient pathway: Since an empath is naturally very intuitive due to their heightened sensitivity, clairsentience is the psychic pathway that becomes their strongest suit. This pathway focuses strongly on emotions, energies, feeling different physical sensations, and this is how the empaths are most likely to channel their energy in a productive way.

However, this might not be the only pathway they are adept at, as some empaths also tend to have great expertise in accessing clairvoyance and/or clairaudience- through which they can either see intuitive guidance in the form of images in their mind or can hear gentle, intuitive guidance.

With more practice and a conscious attempt to hone their empath energy better, empaths can significantly get better at and more in control of their clairsentience over time.

Understanding Empath Energy

Generally, people think of *energy* as something which needs to be gained and preserved- in one form or the other. However, there is more to the term 'energy' when it comes to empaths than what it means to someone who is not an empath, who might think that energy is simply something that we spend and restore periodically.

Empaths are affected by both seen and unseen, identified and unidentified, sources and forms of energy. While most people can only see energetic bodies, empaths can *feel* them and connect better, as they are fundamentally energetic beings. Empaths recognize not just exchanges between people but also the flow of energy, which exists beyond simple social interactions, and are invisible to most other people.

An empath can also use the term *energy* to describe how another person feels to them, as they can often sense the 'vibe' a person gives off since empaths have a very strong sense of intuition. Although most people can only connect with each other on a physical- and sometimes emotional- level, an empath goes well beyond that and connects with them metaphysically since they are able to sense the energy people bring with themselves into any setting.

Understanding Empath Fatigue

Being an empath is not always very easy. Understanding how to properly channel your empath energy takes time, practice, and a lot of self-reflection. It is an exhausting task, and it often leads to a condition known as 'empath fatigue,' which tires an empath out and drains them of their potential to pick up on energies as usual. Here are a few things which empaths need to keep in mind in order to be better in touch with their energy, especially when they feel like they are nearing a stage of long-drawn exhaustion or fatigue –

1. **A deep sense of purpose:** We are often expected to have very superficial things that drive our sense of purpose, but as an empath, it might often feel very draining to have to live up to very broad, almost unrealistic expectations such as "taking care of everyone" or "healing everyone around you." If you are an empath, you will have to understand that there is only so much you can do, and you will need to cleanse yourself of any conditioning which leads you to think that you can achieve the literal impossible so that you can identify a deeper sense of purpose in life.

2. **A clear distinction between empower and enable:** Much of the caregiving work we are taught to take up is focused on enabling and not empowering (the person who is receiving the care). However, as an empath, if you do not equip yourself to use your energy in a way that empowers other people, then the same people would come back to you again and again for help as they would not know how to deal with their issues on their own. This is why it is crucial that empaths take an approach focused on empowering (which involves taking care of oneself and learning to heal on one's own)

others when they take care of them and provide them with any sort of guidance.

3. **Focus on separation and not oneness:** The focus during any spiritual exchange is often placed on the idea of 'oneness.' However, if you are an empath, the chances are high that this aspect is something you already have covered due to the energy you constantly experience and channel. Therefore, what you should turn your attention towards instead is the idea of 'separation.' Empaths need to focus on how to identify and maintain the distinction between their own energy and the energy they receive from other people, and then, they also need to separate which concerns need them to intervene and which do not, so that they are better in charge of where they are investing their efforts.

4. **Seeking help:** Empaths are often reluctant to seek help from others as they feel that it is always this responsibility to care for everyone, even themselves. This feeling of excessive self-reliance can often drive empaths to a stage of fatigue as they are allowing themselves to only give- help and kindness and support- into the world without actively seeking any of it back. In order to strike a better balance between what empaths can do for others and for themselves, they need to open

up to the possibility of baring their souls to another person and accepting help from them as well.

Tips to Overcome Empath Fatigue

Now that we have some idea about empath fatigue, let us look at a few things empaths can actively practice to avoid empath fatigue or to heal from it:

Get to know yourself
This might sound like a very obvious thing, but a lot of empath fatigue could be avoided if people were simply more aware of how empaths functioned or channeled their empath energy, as this would allow them to preserve their energy without facing a point of exhaustion.

A lot of frustration and loss of energy can also be caused by failed attempts at trying to understand who we are.

For example, many times, it is assumed that empaths are automatically introverts, so they are suggested to take more breaks and periods of alone time to re-energize. However, without first understanding how you function in particular, if you give in to such generalized pieces of advice, it might do you more harm than good. A lot of your attempts at dealing with empath fatigue would also become counterproductive at the same time.

Also, if you are aware of how your empath intuition works, you can use some of it to develop the best ways to deal with fatigue and exhaustion in the ways that might work the best for you.

There are a lot of pieces of advice out there to deal with- although some of it needs you to keep a relatively open mind if it does not work for you, then there is no point in going at it expecting different outcomes later.

If you have a gut feeling like something might not be a good fit for you, it is the best idea to move on to the next available option. How to deal with empath fatigue, therefore, is a calculated balance of understanding yourself and what works for you and trying out new tips and tricks.

Invest in self-care

Self-care is a necessity in today's world, which is becoming more chaotic and exhausting by the day.

For empaths, self-care becomes even more important as they are constantly being drained of their energy by their conscious and subconscious social interactions. Also, due to high sensitivity to external energies, it might be extra hard for empaths to take time off to tend to solely themselves.

Most of the time, what happens with empaths is that they are too busy catering to other people and their needs, and in this process, they forget to take enough care of themselves.

This is something that needs to change first and foremost so that excessive empath fatigue can be avoided. Empaths need to acknowledge that nobody can pour from an empty cup. If they push themselves to the point of fatigue that they cannot recover from, that would be harmful to themselves and all the other people they are so used to lending a helping hand and caring for. This is where self-care comes in handy.

Thinking of self-care might immediately make us picture spa days and bubble baths, but that does not have to be the case always. In fact, self-care can be anything that feels beneficial and a little indulgent to you, even if it does not fit the bills for others.

Self-care for empaths might mean taking their time out to go for a walk or finish a book or a movie they had meant to catch up on for a long time. The only thing that is important here is making sure that whatever self-care activity is being chosen involves the empath and only the empath. It ensures that they have no choice but to dedicate their undivided time and attention to themselves and get more in touch with their feelings.

Learn to create boundaries

One of the biggest mistakes empaths sometimes make is to allow toxic people around them unnecessarily drain a lot of their energy which could be utilized someplace else.

A lot of people take empath energy for granted and do not reciprocate in any possible way to the assistance and support they are receiving from empaths, and these are exactly the kind of people who empaths need to cut off from their lives- or at least maintain a healthy distance from- so that they are not constantly experiencing fatigue from only giving and not receiving anything.

Many a time, people with such draining behavior might realize their mistake and might even actively try to change their pattern of interaction, in which case the empaths can make an intuitive decision on how to further their exchanges.

But some people, even after having pointed out their problematic patterns, will continue to take empaths for granted and will shrug off any accountability that might be expected from them.

Such people are often tagged as 'energy vampires' as they suck off energy constantly without any return, and one of the most effective steps to deal with empath fatigue is severing ties with such people.

This act also counts as self-care because this requires the empath to confront toxic people and prioritize their own selves before the needs of others.

Although this might be somewhat hard and confrontational, the effects of this would be long-term and would ensure a lot of additional peace and comfort for the empaths.

Identify your triggers
As an empath, it is essential for you to know what exactly your triggers are. Since there can be many different kinds of empaths, the triggers for all would be very different from each other, and the way in which these triggers need to be dealt with would also be different.

Since no one size fits everyone, empaths need to work on themselves and identify what kind of an empath they are, what triggers them (and how), and how they could possibly deal with these triggers.

Some empaths could be 'physical empaths.' For them, the physical needs of others would take precedence over other requirements. This implies that they might be quite triggered if they are exposed to physical pain and hardships, especially when they are nearing exhaustion.

On the other hand, plant empaths are more likely to feel very deeply connected to nature and everything related to it, and for them, a common trigger could be being cooped up in a built environment for too long a period of time.

A walk in nature can help them cope with longer periods in an urban, indoor setup.

Identifying what your exact triggers are might be very challenging at times, as they are very emotionally loaded signs which you need to identify rationally.

In order to do this, you can try and turn your natural empath intuition inwards, which will help you pay close attention to your inner workings and how they are affected by things that are happening around you, which might give you some sense of the triggers you could be exposing yourself to, even unknowingly.

What goes in also goes out

This is another more commonsensical advice, but this strongly holds true for empaths- good things come out only when good things are going in.

In terms of dietary needs, empaths tend to be a lot more sensitive when it comes to certain stimulants, such as sugar, caffeine, and alcohol.

This is because many empaths are already highly aware and somewhat tightly-wound people who, when exposed to external stimulants, might be driven towards an uncomfortable sensory overdrive.

Often, when exhausted, it might be an easy and convenient idea to turn towards sugary snacks and other junk food to momentarily relieve you of the fatigue you are feeling.

However, this has a lot of adverse consequences if continued over a prolonged period of time.

This holds true because the exhaustion an empath faces is different from normal tiredness and cannot be easily cured by a sugar rush or anything similar.

It does not stem from just a bad night's sleep. Instead, it comes from the empath depleting their inner energy. Until and unless certain inwards functionings are addressed, this fatigue would not be cured in any way, and short-term measures might prove even more harmful for the empath as they might give rise to unhealthy coping mechanisms.

This does not, of course, mean that an empath has to completely cut down on any forms of sugar or caffeine, etc. They just need to make small, mindful changes to their normal diet and especially to the resorts they turn to when they are having a bad day so that they do not take the aid of external stimulants to address fatigue caused by inner energy.

Empath and Psychic Abilities

Chapter 5:
Everything You Need to Know About Psychic Protection

Do you sometimes feel that something is invading your energy? Such an experience can be uncomfortable, intrusive, and sometimes even frightening. It is in these instances that you need psychic protection. In this chapter, we will go over everything that you need to learn about the art of psychic protection in a step-by-step manner.

Psychic protection often revolves around setting up mirrors or shields that will send the negative energy right back at the perpetrator. There are other methods as well that involves the usage of light of different frequencies, and most importantly, white light that not only protects but also purifies.

And there are others who prefer relying on angels and guides who can provide them protection during a psychic attack. But in this chapter, I will show you how you don't need any of these things but protect your psyche through some other methods like strengthening your auric boundaries and setting your chakras right.

When you are under a psychic attack, it means that a certain part of your energy field was open to infiltration. You need to close this energy door or raise the drawbridge so that you can protect yourself from the attack.

An interesting fact that is noticed by experts is that when someone has strong energy boundaries, they usually don't require any psychic protection in the first place. I am not saying that they do not face any challenges or their life is just perfect.

It's not that, but at the same time, they are not victims of psychic attacks.

This shows that the need for protection doesn't arise if you are able to contain your energy. This ensures that your energy is not available and individuated for a psychic attack. And in this way, you are able to break out of the cycle of victim and perpetrator.

But how can this energy containment be made successful? One of the ways is by setting your chakras right. You can also take part in grounding and centering practices to strengthen your energy boundaries. Read on to learn more about these techniques.

Centering and Grounding Exercises

Whether you want to manage your stress levels or protect yourself from psychic invasion, centering and grounding exercises can be really helpful. In fact, whenever we refer to any energetic or spiritual practice, these two things go hand-in-hand.

Once you practice these exercises, you will feel the flow of energy through every part of your body, and you will also gain better control of this energy. Ultimately, these exercises help bring a sense of stillness or peace from within. Another importance of these exercises is that they make you aware of your physical, emotional, and psychic boundaries so that you can easily build your energy shields and effectively engage in psychic protection.

If you follow my advice, I'd recommend that you perform these exercises every day –good practice would be to do it for 15 minutes right after you wake up and another 15 minutes before you retire for the day and go to bed.

There are plenty of ways in which you can practice centering and grounding, but for a beginner, the best way to go about it would be to practice breathing exercises.

What is Grounding?

With the hectic schedules that we all have, it's very easy to get caught up in all the things that you have on your to-do list for the day. And then there are the uncertainties of the future. All of these thoughts often pull a person far away from their present life. That is where grounding comes in.

Through the process of grounding, you can pull yourself back to reality and help yourself connect with the present. It will instantly remind you of the importance of being in the present moment so that you are always aware of the happenings around you and stay conscious.

On days when you feel exceptionally detached from everything that is going on at present, grounding exercises can really shift your focus and bring you back to the here and now. It also teaches you to be mindful.

How to Ground Yourself?

The grounding exercise is pretty easy, and you will get better at it with practice. Start by choosing a place to sit down where you will be free of any distractions. Then, close your eyes. Start taking deep breaths. When you are breathing in and out, focus on your breathing and be mindful and aware of every inhale and exhale that you do.

After a while, you will feel ready and then start visualizing the energy from your body gathering at the center and going down into the ground. You can do this by imagining a network of roots growing from your body and that go further deep into the ground, and they carry the energy with them. The more these roots grow, the more you will feel heavy because they are pulling you into the ground.

If it feels overwhelming, you can simultaneously visualize your spirit being pulled more and more towards your body. After a while, you will feel completely relaxed because now, your spirit and body are one. The next step you need to take is centering.

What is Centering?

Now that you have a basic idea of what grounding is, let us have a look at the next concept, that is, centering. For that, imagine this situation –

You follow your daily schedule and go to work, and the entire day, you are trying your best to keep your boss happy and maximize client satisfaction. You interact with so many people during your shift, and during the entire time, you put on your happy face.

But there are many instances where you have a grumpy client/customer to deal with, and they have a very unpleasant behavior. By the time your day ends, you feel tired and exhausted not only physically but also mentally, and all you want to do is sit in front of the TV or watch some Netflix with your favorite snacks.

Does this sound something like your daily routine? It does to me! And this is also why it is important for every single person to practice centering.

Energy is a universal thing – everything that you see on earth has energy present in it. As you traverse life, you give away some of your energy and keep collecting some energy from others. This exchange of energy should not be left unmonitored. You need to keep track of it somehow; otherwise, soon, you will find yourself feeling overwhelmed due to the negativity of others, and this will start hampering your own soul.

When you practice centering, you bring back the energy that you had initially passed on to others. At the same time, you also shed away the energy that you had collected from people you met. The beneficial nature of this process is that it helps you restore the balance of energy in your body so that you can function more smoothly and effectively without feeling weighed down by something.

How to Center Yourself?

The first thing that you need to know before you center yourself is where your energy center is. There is a breathing exercise that you need to do, and before I explain the steps, there's something else that I need to tell you. When you perform the centering exercise, your aim would be to imagine the energy gathering inside your body in the form of a golden ball.

Centering is usually about your naval area. That is why when you breathe in, it is advised that you do it through your diaphragm. But if you do not yet trust yourself regarding such clear visualization, you need not worry – you can simply imagine the energy flowing to any area it wishes to flow to.

Developing or unlocking your psychic abilities has often been related to the power of visualization and so never put a barrier to your imaginations. When you make the best use of your imagination and wield it purposefully, you acknowledge the presence of energy inside you and eventually learn to silence the inner critic to make the best use of your psychic abilities.

So, start by closing your eyes and take deep breaths. You have to put your visualization to use when you are breathing in – imagine all the energy that you have given out into the world and imagine it coming back to you. As the energy comes back and fills you up, it will make your soul feel complete, and you get a feeling of fullness from within.

Consequently, when you exhale, you need to imagine that you are throwing away all the energy that you had absorbed from others. Imagine this excess rubble inside of you and then simply blow it away. This process will ensure that all of the negative energy blocking your energy flow is now sent away, and your body is neutralized. You feel free and lighter than before.

If you are facing trouble doing, here's an example of a visualization that you can do while performing the breathing exercises. Imagine your energy center and compare it with that of an empty cup. Imagine that the cup is surrounded by a lot of litter. Whenever you inhale, imagine the litter going farther away and your cup being filled with clean water. The water signifies your own energy and the litter – others' energy that you don't want. Or, you can also imagine a garden. With every inhale, visualize new flowers blooming in it, and with every exhale, imagine the weeds being uprooted.

Empath and Psychic Abilities

Conclusion

I wrote this book for anyone who is willing to learn more about psychic empaths and how to make your life easier and your interactions with others more effective by mastering your psychic abilities.

Many of us think that we probably have psychic powers, but we don't know how to hone these skills. I hope this book has helped you to achieve that and assisted you in forming a clear intuition.

Obviously, there are going to be people who are more psychic than others. Some people learn to live with it naturally, whereas some have to develop the skills. But now that you know about the techniques that you can follow, I hope you start embarking on the journey of measuring your psychic powers and making the best use of them.

Printed by Libri Plureos GmbH in Hamburg, Germany